CONTENTS

GW00726138

*

INVOCATION

The flaming blood on my tongue descends
I mix it there with earthly sense

This way I kindle inspiration
From on high. My recitation

Can thus be likened to a spirit
Burning incense in my mouth. Listen!

FLOWER

Images create desire,
Words fix it,
Poetry ends it.

For poetry is the flower
Of words
That burst the bud
To die.

There is but one flower
One poem.
This is the Living Word,
The Flower
That does not die
But lives
By dying
Beyond dying.

Can you taste the incense
Of this sad sweet sacrifice?

If you can
You are a bud
On the Tree of Life:
I AM.

CROSS

Towards death the body slouching,
Towards birth the spirit mounting.
This child is father of the man,
He forms the words of which I AM
But leaf upon His Tree of Life,
His Godly breath to end my strife,
His Angel hands to draw me high
The Cross to spirit-land.

MEDITATION

The Well that I AM
Is infinite, whole and holy.
Into it flows the great
River of Time
In which the multiplicity of Being
In ever changing forms
Finds its own unique expression.
From Me springs the Water
That sustains all life.

I AM a Fountain that flows from heaven,
A draft of divinity.
I AM dark and mysterious
Like the Womb of Night.
And out of my reflective, moonlit waters
Is born the splendour
Of the sun at dawn
Whose golden rays reach out
Like the arms of God
To embrace you in a love-lit joy
On this glad new day.

You are an island in this great
River of Time.
I AM: The Other shore.
The sea of My infinity
Comes to rest

In the Being of our meeting.

There upon the reflecting Water's surface
Where the barque of your life's destiny
Sails amidst the tempests
Of Time's eternal onward flow –
I AM: The starpoint of your tranquillity,
The compass-point of your direction,
The calming deep breath that flows
Beneath your water's heaving, swelling surface.

Seek Me!
Come to Me!
Carry the cup of your life
To this Water's edge and sit with Me.
Turn away from the coarseness of your restless
world,
From its aridity, its crudeness and its savagery.
Sit here quietly.
Look into this Well. Look out upon this Sea.
For here you find the living Water of Life.

Come to Me!
Drink!
I AM: The fullness of your cup.

I AM

The me that you see
Is not the Me
I AM
Or wish to be.

This me is someone else
That seeks to be
I AM
The One you see –

This is the One
I wish to be;
You are
At one with me

If seeing me
You see yourself
I AM
Then one with Thee.

REJOICE!

From womb to tomb
Our lives proceed –
A holy ash from heaven;

We fertilize
The planet Earth,
Divinities creating.

But stained by sin
We failed and fell,
Unfinished and forsaken,

Then He rolled away
The Stone of Death.
Rejoice! We are forgiven.

The Night was long
But Day now breaks;
For this we have been waiting

For aeons past,
But now at last
Fulfilled all expectation.

The Holy One
Informs us now;
All words His Voice in-spoken,

Our partner in
The cosmic dance –
Our mutterings Love's token.

Rejoice! Rejoice!
I say it trice:
Rejoice in Love's creation,

The Earth has now
A star become
And we this star's oration.

Christ is rising
In our hearts.
Let lips become His trumpet

And every ear
With music pierce:
The sweet blood of his drumbeat.

For soon no eye
No heart nor brain
Will fail before His coming;

Even the birds
Will speak His words
And the bees His happy humming.

I AM the Way,
The Truth, He says,

And Life, oh Life abundant;

Who fails to turn
His gaze My Way,
Let him be made redundant.

Oh happy heart
Who hears My words,
To you My Life I'm giving.

Awake beloved
From the dream
As Mary woke from weeping.

Easter is
Reality,
No greater truth can be

Ever known to
Humankind –
Of this your Angel speaks.

So make a place
For Him within,
And go your way with courage;

Uprisen from
Earth's weight you'll be –
Reborn into His entourage.

STAR OF REBIRTH

What is our death
But a last puff of breath
Thrust from the body
Imprisoned of Earth,
The spirit released
To seek out the star
Revealing this secret:
I AM: You are.

GRAIL

Let us have done
With the politics
Of petty hatreds
Of war, death, and division.
Let us light instead
The time-bomb of Love
And let its holy shrapnel
Stealthily pierce
Every separate body
So that in this bleeding
We may drink and eat
Commune and consume
Our new spirit-sweet wine
All pain poured out
Into one shared Cup:

The Grail
Of our transformation.

THE HEALER

Smoothing the rough
Edges of our destiny,
Moving invisibly
Like an Angel
Through the sick,
Casting a dim light
On a dark path
The Healer walks
Among us
Revealing in tiny movements
The Way
To a long promised
Wholeness.

RAPHA-EL* 1

God of thieves and racketeers
Of arts and crafts and many spheres
On Earth, in heaven, and below the shades,
The friend of Man in all his grades -

I hear your voice, I know you well,
    Angel,
        Teacher,
            Rapha-el.

El is an abbreviated form of the Hebrew word elohim donating hierarchical, creator Beings. In these poems the syllable should be emphasised in names where it appears.

WORDS

In among all your words
I listen for the one
That drops like a golden penny
Into the well of my soul
Adding yet another touch
Of star-sparkle
To my collection
Which I keep
In the jewelsafe
Of my spirit-self.

SILENCE

Silence is Power!
But only when it is married
To the Form that emerges
From its unfathomable depths.
This is the Form
Given to the Word
By the angelic Exusiai,
The Word that is no mere word,
No sound wasted
Upon the vanities of time.
No!
This is an Other-Worldly Power
Born deep within the Well of Silence
The Heart of the World.
And it is spoken only through those
Who by Grace are bequeathed
The Gift of the Living Water.
For this is the visionary Power
Of the *Living* Word.

THY BODY - OUR BODY - WE EAT

Each day we live
Each meal we eat
Brings us nearer
To our crossing.
If this be holy
Then holy too our eating.
For in Thy Body
Crossed with Death
We eat us
Thy Earth-fallen Spirit
So that It may be
Ours to grow.

And if this
Our Body's eating
Be our dying too,
Then it in us
Is raised in Thee –
The heavenly scented Flesh
Made full and holy
Through this the incense
Of Thy Spirit Word.

BREAD

If we reach for the stars
From the dust of Earth
Each grain of it will sparkle
In the light that penetrates our soul
Embraced are we by God's sweet Love
Our life his very drink and food
And our dirt the Bread of Masters.

LORD OF THE FULL CIRCLE

In the depths of the night
Has your Cup touched my lips?
For I awake
Scented, warmed, and moistened
By the magic breath of Love,
In-flaming,
And ready to be robed
With yet another coloured day
Wingéd with it from head to foot
Like Hermes,
Ready to glimpse from its horizons
Yet another glorious summit –
To be lifted towards,
To be nourished by,
To be filled with.

UNTITLED

To give and receive
Love and affection
Freed from the flesh-demanding
Pound of possession.

This is a noble
Art to pursue;
The soul growing mightily
Christ-imbued.

RESOLVE:

I will make my body
Strong enough to contain
The joy that sometimes
Threatens to engulf it.

Is this your Body, Lord?

RE-MEMBER:

How can an old man
Act properly
While the child leaps up
In his heart
With a force greater
Than his body?

AN ANSWER:

With an ear cleansed
To the patient virtue
Of a Master,
The Living Word
That bubbles up
From the world's depths
Shapes itself
To an answer.

THE MYSTIC'S ART

In the perfected technique
Of becoming, of centring
And dissolving being
Into cloud or bird or tree,
Self-buried and seeing only
The One Hand everywhere –
The body's rich treasury
Of senses sacrificed
With Him gazing in spirit
On the blazing pearl of God's Kingdom –

In this lay the mystic's art.

SPIRIT CHILD 1

When the Child swells up in me
He pushes himself outside of me
Extending the limits of my reason.

When he stirs in the womb of my soul
I am not old but brought close again
To a new beginning; my thinking is

Cut down to size as if ringed
By a kind of magic only a child
Can bring. 'Be not afraid of me'

He cries as I test and taste
The fissures that fan through my mind
Faithfully trying to embrace this spirit presence

Dropped like a shining stone from heaven
Into my placid pool and centring
Where my innards ripple to his ringing

And hands are gripping and squeezing
The images receding for meaningful words
To conquer the fear of illusion.

But no words can kill this child in me.
He only grows with each new-dawning sun
And I thrill to his lovely innocent coming.

The affirmation then of a virgin birth
Can only be this:
Images conceive it
Words feed it,
Blood and water feel it.

Now hear it!

SPIRIT CHILD 2

I AM a bud upon your tree
A shoot upon your vine.
I AM the sap from which you're made
The water in your wine;

My life's a flame, it burns for you,
My moment's joy and peace
Your ecstasies my days become,
I long for your release.

For you I wait with open arms
And heart and mouth and ears,
Each syllable I write for you –
The offspring of my years,

A child not made of flesh and blood,
A dream-child spirit-free;
I see you come all swaddled up
In the coils of my memory.

You are the Godman, me the child
And Mother Earth our home,
And heaven our sweet Destiny.
Come. Together we will go.

Though lonely while I do not see
You clearly, touch your face,
The joy of waiting for your touch
When I am laid to rest

Sustains my bones upon this Earth
Gives hope to all my trials
That you the Judge will set me free
When my mortal coil expires.

So leap with joy within my heart
You child of spirit-love,
Take shelter here under my roof;
I AM one who'll share your load.

Our lives entwined we'll face the cold
Dispelling doubt and fear;
We'll feed ourselves on Beauty's food
And draw the Father near.

Our Trinity will thus be sealed,
Our living hope complete;
All tasks fulfilled and Peace to reign
When Him at last we'll meet.

OUR BLEST

You are my very essence consecrated in the world
I take from you, I make with you
New words:

Where I have walked and gloried in the summer-scented blooms
You walked with me, you talked with me,
Our tune

Still echoes there where the dappled dancing leafy light
Peeped through for us; you show to us
Your flight

Where a hundred thousand insects weave a shimmering tapestry.
Such playfulness! Your ways for us
Are seen

Wherever earth-sap lifts us up to greet the throbbing day.
Embracing you, we trace for you
The Way

Whereby our lives can chalice-like be lifted to the stars.
Your will for us can fill us up.
We are

A few who hope and watch and wait and listen for your Voice;
We seek with you, we speak with you;
Your light

Can only shine into our lives when hearts and thoughts combine;
So join with us and find in us
The time

To make your Coming manifest; new words to heal the Earth –
Rise up in us, come sup with us
Our Blest.

KARMA

Paradise cannot be seen
For if it were our hearts would bleed
To death with sorrow for this world
We are condemned to live in. Thus
Our eyes are covered with a veil.
We cannot see from whence we came.
We are protected from such bliss.
Each life and limb is ruled by this.

MAYA

The flickering play of sensual awareness
Is but the coloured Veil of Isis
Whose beauty yet no man has seen
Upon the Earth, save in a dream

Or glorious vision like the shepherds had
When they were singled out by God
To make it known that the Queen of Heaven
Who, as humble, pure, and gentle maiden

Had brought into the barren Earth
In darkest hour ethereal light
That eye and sense might penetrate
These veils that cloud our fallen state.

SHINE!

De-light of angles
Surging through my soul.
The light of God
The flame of old

Moving mysteriously
Through this dying place
Creating from our bowls
A God-wrought state,

Borne by their flying
Swimming in their foam
I AM their handiwork
They are my home;

A brick in their temple
I am happy to be,
But happier still
Their faces to see.

Home of my Angel
Body of mine,
Eat me and drink me,
Shine, shine, shine.

RAPHA-EL 2

Being
You
Rapha-el.
I want.
I wait,
Hoped in whit whiteness
For the healing
Tinkle tingle
Of the bell-spirit
Birdsong
Crossing
You
With the plumed plucked
Branch,
Strength
Of the pilgrim feet;
Magic wand
Of my godness;
Word perfect
Praying
And piercing
The veil
Between us.

RESURRECTION ROSE

I offer you
As a gift
My naked self
Stripped of all conditions.

Nail me
To the black cross
Of your dead past
Where our mingled blood
May flow
Like two streams
Into one heart,

Then out from our lips will grow
When we have healed
Our thornéd wounds
The Resurrection Rose

THE BUDDHA'S FLOWER

What keeps you going?
Is it music or love,
Or maybe the jewel-spangled
Heavens above?

Is it sex
Or is it drugs,
Or perhaps its simply
Drinking pints in pubs?

What gets you up
And interested
To live another day of it –
The creepy crawly crazy journey
To the dead
And very end of it?

I'll tell you my secret!
Its simple and true,
(the source of my ecstasy)
And its got nothing to do
With politics, profit
Art or romance,
Fat cats or poor ones
Football or dance……..

I simply remember

The Buddha, whose power
He held up to the world
In the form of a flower.

WORDS, WORDS, WORDS.

Books?
Psshhh!
Something to do with the eye
Or maybe the brain,
Nothing more –
A mere matter of knowledge
As useless as old dry bones
If they do not instruct
On the acquisition of Wisdom
Or help shape into a Godly image
The pure matter of the heart.

IN LOVE

Ah……….saint.
What is this you are doing now?
Crying, laughing, or what?
You are in love again!
With the blueness of the sky
The fullness of the wind
The generous hiss of the rain……….
All human feelings
Purged of mere humanness.
It is the pure
God-kiss of Nature.
She is everywhere!
You cannot hide
From this ecstasy –

You are in the grip of holiness.

ON VISITING ST. KEVIN'S CELL

*(St. Kevin's Cell is located in the early Celtic Church's
monastery, in Glendalough, Co. Wicklow).*

I

All the rich ambrosial peace
You gathered here!
Away from your brothers' bustle
You prayed and watched
The lake and hill
Respond to each angelic touch
Transforming black deliciously
Into shapes and shades
No one but you has seen.
Suffused, your soul melted
Into the flickering beauty
Of Time's slow sad turning.

And all your brothers' love
You held in one clear thought
Perched high above them here
One step nearer to Him
Who flooded your innocent face
With soft tears
When you heard Him
In the deer's gentle rustle
Or saw Him
In the honeyed glint of light on lake.

And as He touched your holy hands
Upheld in ecstasy
In the glistening rain,
Your face shone like the sun.

II

Do you come here still?
Or have you shunned
This place you hallowed
Now bustling with gapers
And screaming children,
A spectral helicopter hovering
In the mad mocking air.

Oh, please come back to this place!
For here is a prayer in the making
One fashioned from our times' struggle,
A time squeezed dry
Of purity and innocence
A deep buried anguish rumbling,
A thin voice crying
For the holy Peace
That you have salvaged.

Oh! Can you pour it out
For us now
Into our desolate souls
At this raging climax of time!

(Easter, 1996)

MICHA-EL

I AM:
The red-hot
Iron-flame
Of your soul
Poured into
Your dying
Body-mould.
Forge therefore
For your own hand
My deathless
Spirit-sword.

BOUND FOR SKELLIG MICHAEL

Skellig Michael is the name of a tiny island in the Atlantic off the southwest coast of Ireland. It was a hermetic, monastic settlement of the Celtic/Christian monks in the 6th century.

There was no doubt
In their minds
Of the Incarnation.
For they were seers!
They knew the secret
Of fallen flesh
Of raised rock
Of Sun and Cross.

Long before the Good News
Of an Earth sanctified
Reached their ears
They were explorers
Of those luminous inscapes
Where the soul's beauty thrives
And Man's mystery
Yields to the inner eye.

They expected transformation!
And when confirmed
Nothing mattered but
The re-born spirit-life

And the search for living symbols
To swell the soul's parameters
That they might feel His Presence
More real than the spirit
Of these heaving thundering waters
That bore them and bound them
To this shimmering Island
Piercing high above ancient Atlantis,
This Rock of courage
Fortress of Micha-el.

These were the first children
Of a new Sun God
Joyfully upraised to a life
Free from all death-dealing
And dark worship,
Plying their way heroically
Through the strife and coarse abandon
Of elemental passion, blood-battles
And land-locked tribal powers,
Riding mighty waves
In their little boats of prayer
Drawn by the great Archangel
To this place where they
Might bring to ever greater life
The Living Word
Imprinted now forever
On the soul of fallen
Sinful warlike Man.

Their sanctuary was built of stone
High upon this Rock
Whose million fingers
Point triumphantly heavenward,
Each step of their stairway
A precious work of love
No kiss could ever equal,
For they were tending
The Body of their Lord
Who drew ever closer
To their aching hearts
With the fabulous passing
Of each new sunrise sunset,
As inch by inch
They wrenched themselves free
From the frail body's mortal toil
And the spirit of their beloved God
Indwelt ever more securely
Until at last there was nothing left
But the martyr's wish for death
That they might stand
Re-born, proud, strong and joy-filled,
Resurrected spirits of a new world
Built of love and lit
By this glorious light
That filled their little hearts
Yet longed to engulf the World –
The light of the Risen One,
The Universal Prince of Peace.

THE LADDER

Why seek any other plane
Except that of the saint?
For at best they are
But hills or plateaus
Whereas his, like God,
Is always rising.

CROSSING

O Lord
Prepare us well
For our meetings
And our crossing with you.
Put us often through the mill
The water and the fire
Of your will to clean us
Your grain thus to sprout
Our spirit so strong
That we will not die
Of the joy of your flesh, flower fresh
And dew-drenched in the sun,
But rise powerfully
To a new life of Light
Transcripted from this troubled Earth
This dark genesis
Of our body of clay
And into the transcendent pasture
Of Your spirit-soul.

OLD KNIGHT

I am the light
In the ice-cold cave.
Charged by virtue
I melt a passage
Through the dark.
My enemies are unpoisoned
By my purifying heat –
They strike in vain
Against my shield.
I glide through the splinters
Of the evil world
Like a knight of old,
The balsam of my pity
Anointing the wounded everywhere;
And my colours shine inwardly
All the brighter
As I draw nearer
To the heart of their sickness;
And through the shared Death of their King
My tired old body is crossed
By the risen Light
And visible Hope
Of all.

ZEN JOY

Practise emptiness!
Be
Like the silent vase
At the window
Still
Awaiting
The hours
The water
The flowers.......

And the sun.

WE WILL NOT DIE..........

............for He has given us
the Cup of His own New Life
which when we take
there lives in us
a substance so sublime
we can hardly bare to think
preferring rather to bathe
in It's glowing warmth,
in It's peace
which knows no name............

PARZIVAL: YOU ARE A GOOSE!

'Before him, in a linden tree, sat a maiden whose
faithfulness in love had brought her great distress'.
Wolfram's Parzival, 249.

Oh foolish youth,
Give up your thoughtless ways!
Get out into the world
And lift your shining eyes
Above the dusky forest
Of your gathering days.

Go seek that Path
To where the Virgin weeps
And fill your thirsty heart
With grief and pain and love
Of her. Listen. She is wise
And she will set you free.

Her love is chaste
Yet warmer than the sun.
If once you rested in her lap
You'd ne'r again be passion's child
And every ache she'd sooth
And heal your every wound.

You'll know her when
You've learned to love the stars
And find her by that rosy light
She holds like an Easter flower
In the crescent
Of her moon-soft arms.

Remember her
When darkness drowns your days
And battered though your armour be
And limbs all limp from toil,
The veil of Death she lifts for you,
Reveals the Holy Grail.

LIA-FAIL

Lia-fail is Gaelic for 'The Stone of Destiny', the magical, speaking Stone
reputed to have been brought to Ireland by the Tuatha De Danaan,
a people who colonised and ruled Ireland in pre-historic times.

The happy rock
Smiling peacefully slept.
Why? I dared to ask.
Because I am
The footfall of a god
It said.
Like you
I am shaped and shelled
Into this blissful body-sleep
Where you hear
The life enchanted
Awakening words in us,
The celestial master-mason
Whose hands of wind and wave
Out of the aeons
Patiently forms
Manages and models us elementals,
Happy to hear and speak
Of our enchantment –
Seeing the seed of the new heart
Sprouting in the old soul.

The wings that are in me therefore
I give to you
That words may master me
And sweeten your sleep and mine.

(Allihes, West Cork, May 2002)

ELEMENTS

Flame!
Dance in the fire
Dance in my head
Dance till your many
Coloured tongues have spread
Like a flower opening
In the plexus of my soul.

Water!
Flow through the fire
Till the flame turns to blood.
My head is an ocean
My body is a boat
My heart seeks devotion
Where the stars are afloat.

Earth!
Field where my feet
Go searching in the sun
A flower-bed where body
And soul unite upon
Home to the eagle
And the scorpion.

Air!
Blue breath of heaven
Warm waves on the wind
Ship-clouds for my shaping
Upsoaring on wings
All darkness dissolving
Where the light knows no end.

SOUL

The chrysalis body of earth
Is but the dank
Sleep-dream of the soul
Wrapped seductively
In the flesh-fold of the Mother,
Its womb-vision tunnelled in darkness
And stirring like a serpent-spirit-child
Into a wakefulness
The pinhead point of midnight light
Waiting to be morning-winged
And guided by this luciferic star
Into the ethereal colours
Of its long-awaited flight –
Divine Psyche sun-seeking the eternal Lover
Uncoiling her wounds in longing
For the blissful bosom of her God.

GOD IS LOVE

Q. What is more useful than knowledge
More sublime than wisdom
More desirable than the world?

A. The joy in the joining
Of the lover utterly
With the beloved.

This is the ecstasy we seek.

Only God can give it to us.

RESURRECTION

I await Thee Lord –
For the completion
Of my pilgrimage;
For the release
From my trial;
For the consummation
Of my humble offering.

Only your Death
In my body
Can raise my poor spirit
To such hopes,
To ground me
In such faith
That wins for me
Such sweetness…………

Such love……………….

THE ROSE-CROSS OF PEACE

Break down your false defences.
Take out your suffering heart.
Nail it to the Cross of Love.
Lift it up into the world
And let it speak.
In this way unite
With all your fellow pilgrims,
And in time
Your heart of suffering
Will be transformed
Into the heart of healing.
It is only out of the suffering hearts
Of all the true seekers of the spirit
That the Rose of Peace
Is formed
And its blossoms
Become a reality.

THE SEED OF CHRIST

Make of your limbs a stable
Make of your gaze a star
Make of your heart a manger
And lay the Christ-child there.

Make of your voice a trumpet
And raise it above the throng
And blow with the breath of heaven
The music for which all men long.

Sing out your song in the wilderness
Scatter its notes on the wind,
Say the little Child is crying
Outside: 'Please let me in'.

Tell the world you heard an angel
Sing when he came to see
The little child inside your heart
Sleeping peacefully.

Then open up your stable
And sweep away the snow
Melt the frost upon your windows
And in the dark let your flame glow

And in time your stable walls will
Crumble as your light grows strong
And a Temple for the spirit's birth
Your body will become.

For this is a mighty secret
That all the world should know:
In every heart at Christmastime
The seed of Christ is sown.

THE DOOR 1

Be
The Christ
In me!

Root
In my soul's blood
The slow strength
Of a tree.

Steady
The compass of my spirit
To face
And follow Thee.

Cross
This very day
A door
To eternity.

THE DOOR 2

The stars are windows
In the Temple of God.
The sun is the Door.

Within this Temple
All is light,
So bright you cannot see.
When you enter it is dark!

Within this dark
Your body will burn away.

In pain your true sight will grow.

Then through the flame-filled
Spirit-eyes of angels
The Bright One
Comes to greet you.

THE WAY, THE TRUTH, AND THE LIFE

I AM the Door
You are the key,
My temple stands
In front of thee.

Its windowed walls
Of countless stars
Each one my eye
That sees afar

The pilgrim Way
The pilgrim too,
I AM the Light
That lives in you

That draws you here,
The Shepherd's Voice
This too I AM.
Come hither child

And be nourished
In my temple shared,
I AM the Bread
You are the blade.

Dark world of Death
Down there below
Give form unto
This inner glow,

Remake thyself
Within My Light,
I AM the Resurrection
And the Life

The Vine, the fruit,
The wine, the blood,
The Beautiful,
The True, the Good.

THE ZODIAC

Think I AM the centre
Of a cosmic wheel
Turned slowly by God's loving hands
Through a surging singing sea of light –

On Earth my body's but a seed
Of liquid life-filled dark,
My every pore a portal to a star
Soul-woven on a web of shining rays

And grounded in imagination's play;
My every sense the wonder-work
Of gods and clustered angels
Of whom one came to me himself –

An 'I' to be – 'I AM' –
A centre in the many-mansioned wheel
Whose living pictures, songs and symphonies
I do but dimly see and hear.

But every time I lift my head
And drink the starry milk of night
My centre grows a little more
With the marvellous turning turning slow.

EPIPHANY

The Star of Grace
Has touched my soul,
And as I seek
To give Thee thanks
Upon my knees I fall,

And scribble there
This song of praise
And offer it
With hands upraised
To you my God, my all.

I WANT MY LOVE

I want my Love to be virginal
White as the snows of old.
I want my Love to be spiritual
Liquid and gleaming like gold.
I want my Love to be single
Without others who get in the way.
I want my Love to be harder
Than diamond, more precious than prayer.
I want my Love to be lasting
Like a mother whose womb still enfolds
Every tender compassion and longing
Outlasting the grave's muddy hole.
I don't want my Love to be selfish.
I don't want it ever to hate.
I want her to lead me to Heaven,
Away from this foul-smelling place.

STEPS THROUGH HELL

So you say you've been to Hell.
By your voice I can tell
How your sweetness has survived it.
Please speak to me
The deeps of your hopelessness
The raw wound of your anguish
The terrible evil
You labour to release.
It is my burden too.

Share with me your steps through Hell
And in the light of this communion
We will find the key
To the doorways of redemption.
Courageously I will stand beside you
And share with you a secret balm.

My secret is composure.

Out of the day's machinations
Where hell-hints and heaven-tints
Are mixed a potion in my soul
I am distilled,
Bestilling words that
Catch a glimpse of me
But killing words
That Fire Spirits fear
Because they live in losing me.

Distilled, I am
Savoured with words
That open
My magical healing conduit
To You.

TWO OR THREE

Here where they run
From each other
And from You
Like frightened beasts
Driven to sacrifice
And worship at false alters
By the mad masters of hate and greed,
I pray the warm and wonderful
Swelling flame of Your friendship
Ray out beyond my aching breast
Like a spirit hand,
And 'ere I die
Touch one or two of them alight
That I may gather in your Name
And be made whole and holy
By this joyful sharing,
The healing touch,
The ultimate beneficence
Of You.

THE MONSTER

Come, cast off night's warm blanket
And look this day in the eye
And sharpen up your weapons
In readiness for fight.

Let virtue be your armour.
Put it on and step outside.
Meet the many-coloured Monster
In the traffic and the noise.

Let its flesh be made of plastic,
Let its blood be thick black oil,
Its mouth of a million engines made
With ten steel tails of a thousand miles.

See its breath in all pollution,
Virgin forests for its food,
And see in global warming signs
Of its seething angry mood.

Be not afraid this is illusion,
It's more real than you can believe,
And if madness dares assault you
As you contemplate this scene

It is wise to know this madness
Is the Monster's work, not yours –

If you recognize the evil thing
You are half-way towards the cure

For instability of mind;
The soul needs white and black;
This fuming, coiling, Dragon paints
His colours from the sack

Of all your senses tuned
To the horrors of our time;
See his work in poisoned rivers
And in much more poisoned minds.

Look with pity on this generation
As it scurries to and fro,
Victims to the Monster's greed,
Innocents massacred.

The time has come for action,
There is nowhere you can hide,
The Monster feeds upon your thoughts
And grows inside your mind –

For although his shadow's everywhere
It's with your headlights he is seen,
And the cruel thing you have to bear
Is in your own imagination.

But, brave heart, don your breastplate
Grip your sword and shine your steel;
This Monster's not invicible
Whether in your head or on the street.

Fight him hard with steadfast courage
With an anger born of love
For every flower that he threads upon
For every tree whose fruit goes bad.

Be like the knight whose Lady
Is so beautiful that he
Sees her beauty threatened everywhere
On land, in sky and sea,

Who is filled with love's adventure
Who is fired by thoughts so pure
They penetrate like bolts of light
This Monster and his brood.

So when sweet sleep has left your limbs
And you step into the light
Pin the badge of courage to your heart
Let your armour shine so bright

And angel may be welcome there
To guide your lonely path
Through the forest of these latter days
Cold, angry, bleak and dark.

PEACE BE WITH YOU?

Peace be with you
The Master said
And I drank it in with joy.

Peace be with me
I oft repeat
Ever since I was a child.

Peace be with you.
So simply said!
Who has not heard the call?

Peace be with us.
But where is it?
Oh! It's the hardest thing of all.

PAIN

Peace
Is
The death
Of waiting.

Out of its
Pain
Create yourself.

Life
Is
The living
Of this;

Love
Making
Unending.

THE MEASURING ROD

The measuring rod
That distances our being from God
Is but a snake's length
A pathetic breath
A sick bloody bite of an apple
The luciferic inch or I
Between heaven and earth
Between me and you
Between love and hate
Between good and evil –
The crucial but ecstatic division -
The pain of knowledge.

WHAT IS A TREE?

It is a skeleton
Of boxed, bracketed
And trellised light
A place of enchanted faces
Pierced by birds
Fleshed with green,
A habitat of ghosts
And patient
As an angel.

LEAF

Be the leaf of your dreams
The feather of your spirit-bird
Blowing you whither it pleases.

Sink into this wind
Wrapping you in heavenly thoughts,
Sailing like Garuda
Through the ocean of Time.

Soar above the clouds
Petal of my heart –
I will sail the spheres
And drench myself with starlight!

(Then later),
Down, down, down
You drop me, fabulous bird,
My leaf-body
Upon this page of Earth.

Oh! Let the hobnailed feet
Crush me now!
So that even my dust might escape!

Blow me spirit-bird.
Blow!

Come round again soon.

PERIPHERY AND CENTRE

I AM
Echoed and mirrored
In the passing day
In its teeming sensations
Searching constantly for new light
In the labyrinth
Of painted and dying faces.

Yet why should I feel
Wonder and joy
In the midst of all this?

It is because You are here
Shining invisibly like a sun-centre
Around which all these fragments orbit
Filling me out beyond my narrow self
And into the throb of a greater life
Joining me to the pulse of others.

PRAYER OF A CAPITALIST

Lord
I want to make you my business –
I want to make a business of you!

In all my dealings
Lord
I will take account of you.
I will measure
My profits and my loss
By my charity and my meanness.
You will be the fulcrum
Lord
Of all my calculating,
The scales of my justice.
Your Word
Lord,
Your figure, your angels and your flock –
Let them be the columns
Of my balance sheet,
The products of my company,
The stuff of my advertising.

Let me buy and sell you
Lord.
Let me mass-produce you.
Let me increase your interest
A thousand percent
Every day of my life.

anyone for SPIRITS?

You cannot water the Spirit down.
If you do it loses potency.
God requires a hundred percent;
Leave his fractions to the Pharisees.

THIS TRUTH

Peace is my parting gift to you. John, 14:27

You are in me
I am in You.

O how long must I wait
Before this Truth
Will set me free?

Here in my workshop
I will toil
- this old and tattered coat –
While I patiently weave
My wedding garment
From the throbbing
Colours of your rainbow,
From the gold and silver threads
That web the lovely cosmic canopy
Of silent singing stars.
Then when I hear your call
I will go out
With an aching heart
And pick my way
Along the thorny path
That leads to your secret house.
There I will lose myself
In the glow

Of your all-consuming beauty
And bathe my thirsty soul
In the melody
Of your heavenly Voice.

O joyful friend and comforter,
O sweetest lover
Beyond all death-worship
And impure desire,
Let the draught of living light
That flows from your miraculous Cup
Wash away all my fears
That I may be uprisen, bold,
And victorious against all those powers
That would keep us apart
And confine me here
To the darkness
Of this, my tiny self.

I AM

'The I AM – what does that mean? The I AM is the name for the divine Being, the Christ-principle of man – the Being of whom man feels like a drop, a spark, when he can say 'I AM'. The stone, the plant, the animal cannot say 'I AM'. Man is the crown of creation inasmuch as he can say 'I AM' to himself; he can utter a name which does not hold good for anyone but the one who utters it. You alone can call yourself 'I'; no one else can call you 'I'. Here the soul speaks within itself in a word to which none other has entrance except a Being which comes to the soul through no external sense, on no outer path. Here Divinity speaks. Hence the name 'I AM' was given to the Godhead whose Being fills the world'.

Rudolf Steiner